MARTIAL ARTS
SPORTS ZONE

KARATE

JAPANESE EMPTY-HAND COMBAT

Garrison Wells

D1212961

Lerner Publications Company • Minneapolis

Lerner Publications Company
A division of Lerner Publishing Group, Inc.
241 First Avenue North
Minneapolis, MN 55401 U.S.A.

Website address: www.lernerbooks.com

Content Consultant: Lucio Farías, martial arts Grand Master and founder of International Budokan, Michigan

Library of Congress Cataloging-in-Publication Data
Wells, Garrison.
  Karate : Japanese empty-hand combat / by Garrison Wells.
     p. cm. — (Martial arts sports zone)
  Includes index.
  ISBN 978-0-7613-8459-5 (lib. bdg. : alk. paper) 1. Karate. I. Title.
  GV1114.3.W434 2012
  796.8153—dc23   2011035275

Manufactured in the United States of America
1—BC—12/31/11

Photo credits: Al Bello/Zuffa LLC//Getty Images, 5; Jordan Shaw/iStockphoto, 6 (left); Diether Endlicher/AP Images, 6 (right); Dimension Films/Photofest, 7; John Florea/Time & Life Pictures/ Getty Images, 9 (top); Orlando/Getty Images, 9 (bottom); Kyodo/AP Images, 11, 17; Columbia Pictures/Photofest, 12; Mary Evans/Asian Union Film and Entertainment Ltd/China Film Co Produ/ Ronald Grant/Everett Collection, 13; Dita Alangkara/AP Images, 15, 20; Claude Florent Donne Photographie/iStockphoto, 16; Salim October/Shutterstock Images, 18 (top); Shutterstock Images, 18 (bottom), 29 (bottom); Noah Seelam/AFP/Getty Images, 19; Testing/Shutterstock Images, 23; Roslan Rahman/AFP/Getty Images, 24; Blend Images/Alamy, 25; Zuffa LLC/Getty Images, 27; Vita Khorzhevska/Shutterstock Images, 28; Lora Severson/Fotolia, 29 (top)
Backgrounds: Aleksandar Velasevic/iStockphoto, Patrick Wong/iStockphoto
Cover: © Imago/ZUMA Press (main); © iStockphoto.com/Aleksandar Velasevic (background).
Main body text set in ITC Serif Gothic Std Bold 11/17.
Typeface provided by Adobe Systems.

TABLE OF CONTENTS

CHAPTER ONE

OVERVIEW OF KARATE

In April 2011, the Ultimate Fighting Championship (UFC) held UFC 129. The UFC is a competition for mixed martial arts (MMA). So, in the UFC, various martial arts are in play. In UFC 129, Lyoto Machida knocked out Randy Couture in the second round. Machida used a front karate kick to win the fight.

Lyoto has studied karate since he was three years old. He learned from his father, karate master Yoshizo Machida. Yoshizo is head of the Japan Karate Association in Brazil. Lyoto earned his black belt (a sign of the highest level of skill) by the time he was 13.

Lyoto is living proof of the effectiveness of karate. He used karate's striking and kicking techniques to win the UFC light heavyweight championship.

DEFINING KARATE

Karate is a stand-up striking style of martial arts. Karate includes punches, kicks, elbow and knee strikes, blocks, and some throws.

Lyoto Machida (*top*) delivers the front kick that knocked out Randy Couture in UFC 129.

5

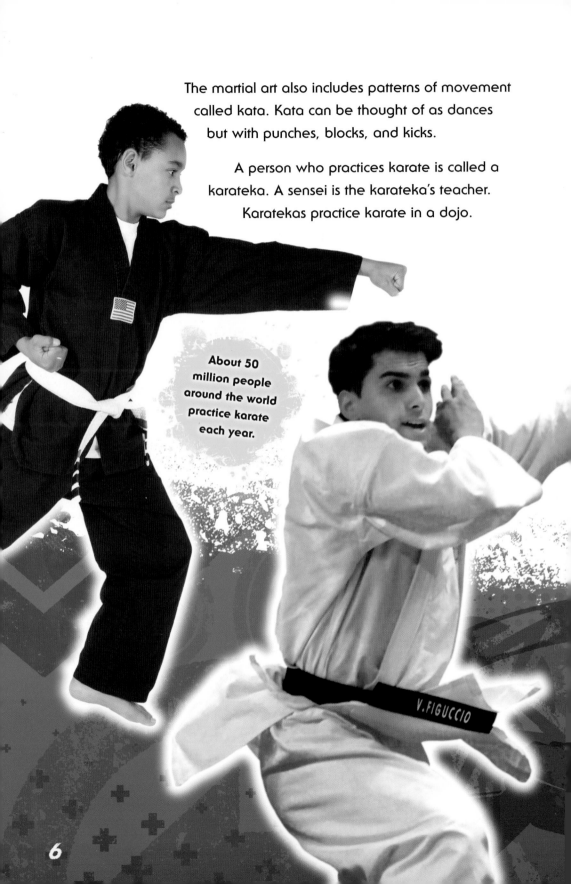

The martial art also includes patterns of movement called kata. Kata can be thought of as dances but with punches, blocks, and kicks.

A person who practices karate is called a karateka. A sensei is the karateka's teacher. Karatekas practice karate in a dojo.

About 50 million people around the world practice karate each year.

V. FIGUCCIO

A dojo can be a basement, a church, or a garage. It can also be a school gym or even a space outdoors.

Karate is for more than fighting. It is a way to learn self-defense while getting in shape. Practicing karate also helps develop self-discipline. This is because a karateka has to work hard to earn a black belt. Karate gives students a way to deal with emotions too. For many, the martial art is a way of life.

CELEBRITIES AND KARATE

MANY CELEBRITIES STUDY KARATE FOR SELF-DEFENSE AND TO STAY IN SHAPE. ACTORS INCLUDE TAYLOR LAUTNER, DANIELLA ALONSO, JENNIFER ANISTON, WESLEY SNIPES, AND FOREST WHITAKER. SINGER ELVIS PRESLEY HAD A BLACK BELT.

Taylor Lautner, of *New Moon* fame, studied karate seriously from a young age. He was able to use those skills in the 2005 movie *The Adventures of Sharkboy and Lavagirl 3-D* (right).

CHAPTER TWO
HISTORY AND CULTURE

Karate developed hundreds of years ago in the Ryuku Islands. These island groups sit at the southern end of modern Japan. Okinawa is the largest of the groups. The word *karate* is Japanese for "empty hand." This means the martial art does not need to be practiced with weapons.

The Okinawans developed karate as a striking art. Immigrants from China influenced karate fighting styles. These Chinese forms remain important parts of modern karate.

In the early twentieth century, an Okinawan named Gichin Funakoshi practiced karate. He created a style known as shotokan. He brought shotokan to mainland Japan around 1920. It quickly became popular at university karate clubs throughout Japan. During the 1930s and the 1940s, Japanese soldiers practiced karate as part of their military training.

Karatekas demonstrate their attacking and blocking skills.

9

KARATE IN THE UNITED STATES

After Japan's defeat in World War II (1939–1945), U.S. soldiers lived in Okinawa and other parts of Japan. There the soldiers were shown karate. Some brought it back to the United States. But the martial art didn't take off until the 1960s, when action movies showcased karate in fight scenes.

Ed Parker also helped spread karate in the United States. He learned a karate style called kenpo while living in Hawaii. This karate style is a mix of several martial arts forms. Kenpo's popularity grew when Parker went to the U.S. mainland. Dojos opened in many U.S. cities.

Choosing a style of karate that is the best fit might take a little research. But finding a place to learn isn't difficult. Karate is often taught in health clubs, gyms, and even in dance schools. Schools teach several karate styles. These include kenpo, Shorin-ryu, Goju-ryu, Wado-ryu, shotokan, and budokan. Many karate instruction DVDs, books, and magazines are also available.

CHINA CONNECTION

Karate's Chinese influence comes from kung fu. Kung fu is similar to karate. It is a stand-up style of fighting that includes mostly punches, blocks, and kicks. Legendary martial artist and actor Bruce Lee trained in kung fu. He is credited with popularizing martial arts through his movies.

Members of the U.S. military practice karate as part of their training.

MOVIES AND TELEVISION

Many movies feature karate in fight scenes, whether or not the story line is about karate. The stories of karate movies and television are usually similar. An underdog has enemies and problems. He or she then rises above them with the help of karate. The stories often include the positive lessons of karate. These include honor, self-esteem, self-discipline, and spiritual and emotional growth.

Jackie Chan (left) and Jaden Smith (right) shoot a scene in *The Karate Kid.*

The Karate Kid movies get a lot of credit for helping make karate popular. The first movie came out in 1984. But altogether five *Karate Kid* movies have hit the big screen. The most recent version came out in 2010. It starred Jackie Chan and Jaden Smith.

In 1990 the first *Teenage Mutant Ninja Turtles* movie was released. The series is about mutated turtles that are skilled in karate. The series also became a popular television show. Several comic books star the teenage mutant ninja turtles as well.

Disney has begun a comedy television series called *Kickin' It* about a group who practices karate. The show stars Leo Howard. Howard has experience in Chinese wushu and karate. He says he wants to be the next Bruce Lee.

Another movie that has drawn attention to karate is *Crouching Tiger, Hidden Dragon*. It was released in 2000. The movie features Chinese martial arts styles that are also a part of karate. The movie helped bring more attention to karate and other striking arts.

Actress Michelle Yeoh *(left)* delivers a karate kick in *Crouching Tiger, Hidden Dragon.*

CHAPTER THREE

EQUIPMENT AND MOVES

Karate is practiced in a uniform called a *gi* that has a top similar to a robe and loose-fitting pants. The gi is usually white. Traditional schools use white to represent purity. Some schools allow students to wear different colored gis. Gi pants can have ties or an elastic waist. A thick belt is also worn around the waist of the gi top. The belt comes in different colors that show the skill level of the student. The gi and the belts are also symbols. Once a student puts on a gi, he or she enters the world of martial arts.

In sparring, two students practice moves against one another. Protection is critical for sparring. Basic gear includes a mouthpiece, head protection, and a groin cup. Other protective equipment includes shin, elbow, and foot pads. Gloves, hand wraps, and chest guards are also used. What a student wears depends on the style of karate he or she practices. The preferences of the teacher also play a role. Some sensei prefer lots of pads, especially for younger students. Other teachers prefer less protection.

Karatekas wear traditional gis, along with padded gloves and footwear, for protection during a sparring match.

Classes take place in the dojo. In an indoor dojo, mirrors help students make sure their form is correct. Heavy bags hang from the ceiling for practicing punching and kicking. Sometimes a sparring partner holds pads for the partner to punch and kick.

MOVES

Karate strikes are done with a fist or the edge of the hands, palms, knuckles, or fingertips. Karate also includes striking with the knees and elbows. Kicks are done with the side, the top, or the ball of the foot, or even with the toes. Toe kicks are done in Uechi-ryu karate.

Karate may seem similar to boxing, but it is different. Karate strikes have specific targets, such as the throat, the eyes, the knees, and other sensitive areas. This is because karate's focus is self-defense.

PUNCHES AND STRIKES

Punches are essential to karate. Lyoto Machida uses the forward punch in his fights. The power of the forward karate punch begins in the legs. It is a straight punch. It uses the knuckles of the index and middle finger. The wrist must be kept straight. If it is bent, the puncher can hurt his or her wrist. Targets include the center of the chest, the front of the face, and the nose.

Legs are used to get a powerful forward punch.

Rika Usami from Japan demonstrated a knife hand at the 2010 Asian Games.

There are several types of strikes. A strike using the side of the hand away from the thumb is called a knife hand. This is effective against the side of the neck and the throat. A reverse knife hand uses the thumb side of the hand to strike. The thumb is tucked into the palm.

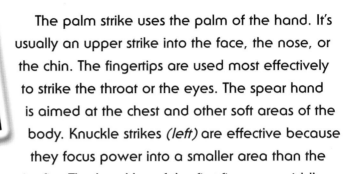

The palm strike uses the palm of the hand. It's usually an upper strike into the face, the nose, or the chin. The fingertips are used most effectively to strike the throat or the eyes. The spear hand is aimed at the chest and other soft areas of the body. Knuckle strikes *(left)* are effective because they focus power into a smaller area than the entire fist. The knuckles of the first finger or middle finger are used to strike soft areas of the body. These include the eyes, the temples, the throat, and the stomach. Another move uses all knuckles extended.

A back fist *(left)* uses the back of the bigger, top knuckles. The strike occurs with the palm facing in. Targets for the back fist include the nose and the face. The hammer fist punch uses the bottom of the fist to strike downward on the face.

KICKS

Kicks are more powerful than punches, have longer reach, and add variety to an attack. The front kick is used for offense and defense. It's done by raising the knee straight up and then extending the leg forward. Striking with the ball of the foot into the chest drives away an attacker. The kick is very powerful. Targets range from the face, the abdomen, and the knees.

India's Valena Valentina performs a front kick during a competition.

The side kick is one of the most powerful karate kicks. It's done by raising the knee, turning sideways, and snapping the foot toward the target. The kick uses either the side or the heel of the foot. The target is usually mid-chest. The roundhouse kick is used to strike the legs, the middle of the ribs, and the head. It gets its name from the way the fighter's leg comes around in a circular motion.

Iran's Jasem Modami Vishkaei (right) blocks his opponent's kick on his way to winning the gold medal at the 2010 Asian Games.

BLOCKS

Karate isn't just about attacking. In fact, it was first developed as a defensive art. Three basic blocks protect most of a person's body. The upper block helps a karateka avoid a punch to the face. The middle block protects against a punch or a kick to the stomach or the chest. The low block shields kicks or punches to the lower half of the body.

KATA

Kata is a series of set moves practiced in a flow, like a dance. But kata is not just for art or beauty. Practicing kata lets a person also practice blocks, punches, kicks, joint locks, and throws. Some masters say that the secret of karate is in the kata. They say through constant practice of kata, karate's secrets will be shown.

The kata of karatekas is also a way for the sensei to measure student's abilities. This lets a teacher know if a student is ready to move to the next belt level. As belt rank gets higher, kata becomes harder and more complex.

WEAPONS

Karate can be done with an open hand and no weapons. However, weapons are a part of the martial art too. Weapons developed during karate's early years. Many were farm tools that developed into weapons. The most common are the nunchaku, the *sai*, the *bo*, and the *kama*. The weapons are not really used anymore. But many people still practice with them. Weapons are often involved in competition.

COMMON WEAPONS

NUNCHAKU: HAS TWO PIECES OF CIGAR-SHAPED WOOD TIED TOGETHER WITH A ROPE, A LEATHER STRAP, OR A CHAIN. THE USER HOLDS ONE PIECE OF WOOD, WHILE SWINGING THE OTHER AT THE OPPONENT. BRUCE LEE IS FAMOUS FOR USING THE NUNCHAKU IN FIGHTS.

SAI: A PAIR OF POINTED METAL STICKS, A BIT LIKE SHORT SWORDS. THEY ARE USED FOR BLOCKING, PUNCHING, AND STABBING. RAPHAEL IN *TEENAGE MUTANT NINJA TURTLES* USES THE SAI.

BO: A LONG STICK THAT CAN BE USED TO HIT OPPONENTS WHEN SWUNG IN CIRCLES. DONATELLO IN *TEENAGE MUTANT NINJA TURTLES* USES THE BO.

KAMA: A WOODEN HANDLE WITH A SHARP, CURVED, METAL BLADE AT ONE END. A PAIR OF KAMA IS USED TO BLOCK, SWIPE AT, AND CUT AN OPPONENT. THE KAMA IS PART OF THE *LEGEND OF THE SEEKER* TV SERIES.

CHAPTER FOUR

SELF-DEFENSE AND COMPETITION

Karate as a form of self-defense gets its effectiveness from its variety of attacks and blocks. Quick punches and kicks coming from all directions are hard for an attacker to escape. Karate differs from fighting styles such as boxing because karate strikes have specific targets. For instance, a back fist can break the nose. A low kick can injure a knee. A knife hand or knuckle strike can seriously damage an eye or the throat.

Karate trains the reflexes. It shows students the correct

ILLEGAL MOVES IN TOURNAMENTS

- TOO MUCH CONTACT
- BITING OR SCRATCHING
- TOO MUCH GRABBING AND HOLDING
- USING DANGEROUS THROWS, JOINT LOCKS, OR UNCONTROLLED MOVES
- USING FOUL LANGUAGE
- ATTACKING AFTER YAME (STOP) HAS BEEN CALLED
- INJURING THE LEGS
- ATTACKING VITAL AREAS SUCH AS THE GROIN AND THE EYES

Karatekas spar at the 2010 SportAccord Combat Games in Beijing, China.

and most effective way to punch, kick, and block. Some styles of karate also include body hardening. Students condition specific points of the body by striking or kicking a padded board called a *makiwara* over and over. When practiced with correct striking form, the makiwara hardens the bones.

Students need self-discipline to earn the top belts in karate. The martial art takes a lot of practice to perfect moves. Students who want to be perfect at self-defense right away may be disappointed. But if they continue with training, their self-discipline will improve.

KARATEKAS COMPETING

Karatekas from around the world compete in local, national, and international competitions. Competitions include events such as kata, team kata, sparring, weapons, and breaking. Divisions are formed by age, rank, and gender.

Sparring has a referee with other judges on the edges of the sparring area. In sparring, there can be light or full contact, depending on the style. The winner is the fighter with the most points. Competitors usually get one point for hitting the opponent's abdomen or head with the fist. They are awarded two points for kicking the abdomen.

Japan's Tetsuya Furukawa performs in a kata competition.

Board breaking is commonly used to test the skill of advanced karate students.

Competitors earn three points for a head kick. In sparring and low-contact tournaments, the punches and kicks are "pulled." This means they are not done with full force to keep from injuring the opponent. Full power is used in full-contact karate tournaments. Competitors win either by knockout or points.

A panel judges kata. Victory is gained by winning the most points and by displaying knowledge of the moves. Students are graded on form, presentation, and level of skill.

INTERNATIONAL COMPETITION

On the international level, the World Karate Federation (WKF) governs karate competition. It is the largest karate organization in the world.

Karate has not yet become an Olympic sport. But in 2005, the International Olympic Committee considered the idea. The sport didn't get enough votes, but it's getting closer to approval.

Major tournaments include the WKF's World University Karate Championship, the Panamerican Senior Karate Championships, and the World Games. The USA Karate-Do Federation hosts the U.S. Karate Championships every year.

UFC AND KARATE

Another way karate is used in competition is in the UFC. Several of these MMA professionals have a background in karate. There's Machida, of course. UFC champion Anderson Silva is another. He used a karate front kick to knock out his opponent in a 2011 fight.

Anderson Silva (right) knocked out Vitor Belfort (left) with a well-placed front kick during UFC 126.

A person can practice karate for competition or for self-defense. Either way, this martial art is a good way to get in shape and learn to protect oneself. Karate has been around for hundreds of years. It will surely be practiced for many years to come.

KARATE HOW-TO

SIDE KICK

A fighter begins by standing with the legs spread a little wider than shoulder width. One side of the fighter should be facing the opponent. Feet are pointed forward. The fighter brings up the hands to the midsection. Then the fighter lifts the leg closest to the opponent up toward the chest while twisting the other leg and foot outward. This prevents hurting the hips. Once the foot is twisted, the fighter thrusts the raised foot out to the side at the target.

ROUNDHOUSE KICK

A fighter begins standing with one leg a little further back than the other. The fighter then bends the back leg and lifts the knee so the leg is tilted very high up. Lastly, the fighter fires out the foot while twisting toward the opponent.

A roundhouse kick

The hand position for a palm strike

PALM STRIKE

A fighter begins by standing with the legs spread a little wider than shoulder width. To prepare the hand for striking, the fighter bends the wrist back as far as it can go. The fighter curls the fingers at the joints and tucks the thumb into the palm. The palm should remain open. The fighter shoots the arm forward and upward, hitting the opponent in the nose or the chin with the palm of the hand.

KNIFE HAND

A fighter begins by standing with the legs spread a little wider than shoulder width. The fighter punches one fist forward while the other hand is brought back to the ear. The hand that is brought back should be open and flat with the thumb tucked against the side. Next, the fighter brings back the punching arm while simultaneously bringing down the knife hand, striking the opponent with the edge of the hand in a knifelike motion.

The hand position for a knife hand

GLOSSARY

ABDOMEN

the front part of the body between the chest and the hips

CONDITION

to train for proper use

DEFENSE

ways of resisting attack

IMMIGRANT

a person, from a different country who comes to a new country to live

MAINLAND

the main part of a country or a continent, rather than an island

MUTATED

something that has been changed on a biological level

OFFENSE

ways of attacking

PULL

to soften kicks and punches to avoid injury

PURITY

free of fault or guilt

REFEREE

a person who judges or guides a sporting event

REFLEX

an instinctive or automatic response to something

UNDERDOG

the predicted loser in a competition

FOR MORE INFORMATION

FURTHER READING

Gifford, Clive. *Karate*. Mankato, MN: Sea to Sea Publications, 2011.

Martin, Ashley. *How to Improve at Karate*. New York: Crabtree Publishing Company, 2008.

Rielly, Robin L. *Karate for Kids*. Boston: Tuttle Publishing, 2004.

Wells, Garrison. *Tae Kwon Do: Korean Foot and Fist Combat*. Minneapolis: Lerner Publications Company, 2012.

WEBSITES

The Black Belt Club
http://www.scholastic.com/blackbeltclub
This interactive website lets visitors build a sequence of karate moves and then watch them be performed.

Kids Ask Sensei
http://www.asksensei.com/kidsQT.html
This site includes more information about karate, including how to tie a belt.

USA Karate
http://www.usankf.org
The official website for karate in the United States, it includes event information, results, and other resources about all levels of karate.

INDEX

ABOUT THE AUTHOR

Garrison Wells is a third-degree black belt in Nihon jujitsu, first-degree black belt in judo, third-degree black belt in Goju-ryu karate, and first-degree black belt in kobudo. He is also an award-winning journalist and writer. Wells lives in Colorado.